Monty and Tyler
Take the Top Road

by

Desmond P.A. Feely

First Published in 2009 by Margon Press Ltd.

Story idea, all text and photography
Copyright © Desmond P. A. Feely, 2009

ISBN 978-0-9563635-0-3

www.montyandtyler.com
www.margonpress.com

Cover photographs and those on pages 41, 47 and 49 courtesy of North News and Pictures. Design and Layout: Commercial Campaigns Ltd.

Dedicated to

Sarah's Mum

"The best mum a daughter could wish for"

In loving memory of my daughter
Corporal Sarah Louise Bryant (*née* Feely)
KIA Afghanistan 17/06/08

All of the animal and human characters in this story are real,
and the stories themselves are true.
I hope you enjoy learning a little about my daughter's much-loved pets,
whilst knowing that your purchase has contributed to alleviating
the suffering of injured veterans in the form of a donation being made
from the proceeds of sale to various war veteran charities including
'Help for Heroes', an organisation I am proud to support.

Part 1: Tyler's new home

Hello! I'm Tyler

Hello, my name is Tyler and I'm a dog – a black Labrador to be precise.

I know lots of humans are called Tyler too, but when I was old enough to understand, my 'new Dad' told me the reason he chose that name for me.

In the olden days of castles, kings, and knights, the soldier on guard-duty outside the castle's drawbridge was called 'a Tyler', which meant he was 'the outer guard' placed at the furthest point from the castle.

The Tyler was a very important soldier because his job was to be the first to spot any trouble so he could raise the alarm.

As I grew up, one of my household duties was to be a guard dog, which is why my 'Dad' decided it was the perfect name for me – not only because I was in charge of guarding the house, but also because I was the most important 'person' in the house.

Leaving Home

The day I became part of a human family was a pretty scary day for me, but it was also exciting. For quite a while I'd been wondering where my brothers and sisters kept disappearing to each time nice people came to visit, so I had no idea how my special day would end – but I thought one thing was certain - I would soon find out!

I remember waking up feeling all fuzzy-eyed on what seemed like just another day, but I hadn't realised that my turn to leave home had finally arrived. As I pottered about my kennel slowly waking up in my usual sleepy little way, my kennel door slowly began to open and a very beautiful girl appeared and bent down to greet me. I was a little surprised at first, but as she came towards me I noticed she had a very pretty face, with long, blonde hair tied back in a ponytail – there was so much love in her eyes and happiness in her smile. Even though I couldn't be completely sure, the sight of this lovely, kind girl made me feel as though I was about to move into a whole new, fun-loving world.

However, there was just one bothersome little distraction amongst all the excitement. There were two men talking and shaking hands – "Hmm, that is a bit strange," I thought to myself! By now the beautiful girl had picked me up and was giving me a lovely cuddle, but I kept stretching my neck to look over her shoulder – I wasn't sure what was going on at all. Then I suddenly realised – one man was giving the other man money – Huh! I'd just been sold!

As things turned out, I shouldn't have been offended. I later discovered that all pups like me are sold. I'm what's called a pedigree, which means I'm from a 'posh dog family' – we're not just very clever but we are also popular working dogs, and have had pride of place in lots of famous houses and farms up and down the land for a very long time.

Doggy Years: one x seven = ?

We dogs, as with most animals, don't live as long as people, and that's why we count about seven years to be the same as one human year. In other words, when I've lived for ten years, I am not really ten years old, but I am more like seventy human years old! So I go from being a puppy to being just like a grandparent fairly quickly, compared to you!

Puppies like me go to a new home when we're only about nine weeks old. It doesn't sound very grown up compared to a human baby, but as I said, I am really seven times older than 'nine weeks', so that would make me one year, two months and three weeks old in human years! That's plenty old enough for a puppy to go to a new home, so don't worry – I'll be fine.

The Journey to my New Home

It seemed like a long journey home – I am not sure how far we drove, but I overheard the humans saying it had taken nearly two hours – to me it felt as though it had taken two days!

I was in the back of the car – a 'hatchback' I think it's called – and the girl that I was hoping was going to be my new Mum was leaning over the back seat and trying to comfort me. I wasn't feeling too well and I think she knew that – she tried to keep me calm and patted my head, especially when we went around a tight corner – well, it wasn't much fun I can tell you! It was okay for the humans – they had something called a seat belt to hold them still, but I couldn't stay on my four paws! I think the pretty girl knew I was frightened because when she saw that I had rolled over once or twice as I tried to get the hang of this new little experience, she reached into the back of the car and held onto me ever so tightly.

I had never left home before, and most definitely had never been in the back of a car. It was really quite nerve-wracking, and you know what happens when little puppy dogs get nervous don't you? Yes, you've guess it – I needed to 'spend a penny', but unfortunately nobody had told me I couldn't do it in the car. By the time we arrived at my new home I had 'spent' quite a few! Not the best of starts for me, especially as it was a brand new car - never mind!

We've Arrived

I heard the car driving slowly on something that sounded crunchy, which turned out to be gravel on the driveway of my new home. The car stopped and suddenly everything was still and very quiet. Just as I was looking around and wondering what was going to happen next, the humans started to climb out of the car and the girl reached into the back and picked me up. I was stretching my neck excitedly to see as much as I could, but just then I heard the man shout, "Oh no!" My little ears flopped and I tucked my head tightly under the girl's arm – "Uh oh," I thought to myself, "the man must have noticed my little 'accidents'!"

I wasn't really told off because I think the man and my new Mum realised that the journey had been a little long and stressful, but as they busied themselves tidying up, I could sort of tell they weren't too impressed and that I probably shouldn't do it again!

When we started to make our way towards the house, I tried to listen in to what they were talking about. They seemed very friendly towards one another, and that was when I overheard the girl saying 'Dad' when she spoke to the man who'd just paid for me. Can you believe that – my pretty new 'Mum' was the man's baby girl! I was quite excited to find out that the man was also part of my new family – he seemed very friendly and I could tell that my new Mum liked him a lot, but one thing did bother me though. The girl seemed quite grown up, and I couldn't understand why she was still living with her Dad and hadn't been sold off just like me.

My Poor Paws

After I'd been lifted out of the car I was put gently on the ground. I tried to have my first little walk on the crunchy stones on the driveway while having a good sniff around the brand new, very smelly car, but oh gosh – that first little walk on those sharp stones was uncomfortable!

I was pleased when the girl picked me up again because there were great big chunky bits of stone everywhere, which had begun to hurt my soft paws – I'd only ever been used to nice dry straw on the ground, so this felt very strange to me! Never mind, the nice girl told me my paws would soon toughen up and I would get used to it after a while.

But for now, I had other more important things on my mind – I could not get over how humans managed to walk with just two legs when I was still struggling with four!

12

Inside the House

As we went inside their kennel - I mean house – the girl put me down on a smooth floor: "That's better," I thought, "no sharp stones here."

Apparently, I was in their kitchen, but I was so excited that I ran off to explore the rest of the house, only to find my paws were now slipping all over the place on the shiny, smooth floor. "There should be a warning sign up somewhere around here," I thought!

Then all of a sudden I realised I could run like mad – now I was in another room where my paws could get a good grip – I think it had what they call a carpet, but whatever it was, I loved it – and oh boy, could I move fast! There were a few things in my way, but that didn't matter - now I could turn on a button and race around at high speed. In fact, within seconds I'd become an expert at travelling at the speed of sound while manoeuvring my way throughout the house, but for some reason the humans didn't appreciate my new-found skill! "Aghh!! Tyler," they both yelled at once.

I could tell my popularity was beginning to wane as they desperately reached out to pick up a knocked-over chair and umbrella stand, but they really needn't have worried – I knew EXACTLY what I was doing, despite how it might have looked!

Who Else Lives Here?

It didn't take long before I realised that I wasn't the only pet who lived here that was cuddly, furry, and had four legs and a tail! 'It' was rather an odd-looking thing, which I soon discovered was called a cat. But for some strange reason 'it' didn't want to play with me – in fact, quite the opposite - it seemed very bad-tempered.

Maybe it had something to do with how we first met? I suddenly heard that funny noise cats make called a 'meow', so as quick as a flash I ran off to investigate. Thanks to the living room carpet, before I knew it I was running at top speed – well, top speed for a puppy!

Then suddenly, I was back on that slippery stuff in the kitchen and skidding all over the place. I was in such a hurry to see what was making the funny noise that I didn't realise I couldn't stop. I suppose crashing into my new four-legged friend like a ten-pin bowling ball was never going to make a good first impression!

As the cat hissed and spat in my direction, the girl thought I might get badly scratched, so she shouted at her to stop. That was how I found out her name was Tweedy, which I thought was a kind of cute name for a furry cat! Tweedy was not terribly keen on me for a while, but when I eventually learned to stop dashing around my new home, she started to be a little nicer.

Tweedy taught me lots of helpful do's and don'ts, as well as the house-rules, some of which I think she'd made up herself, especially the one about which was 'her dinner bowl'!

My Brand New Family

My bed was in the kitchen next to the radiator so I could be kept warm - a special treat that all little puppy dogs deserve! I was very tired after my long journey home, so I didn't wake up until I heard the sound of my new family coming downstairs the following morning. I was very excited to see them and jumped up and down with delight, but almost straight away they led me towards the kitchen door and encouraged me to leave. I began to wonder if I'd done something wrong, until my new Dad explained.

"It's time for you to learn 'the obvious'," said Dad as he followed me outside and put on his wellington boots.

"Hmm, 'the obvious'," I thought to myself, "what on earth is that?"

One of the first things I learned about my new Dad was that he had funny sayings and nick-names for just about everything, and 'the obvious' turned out to be a very important daily routine, which I believe you humans call 'potty training'! When Dad called me to follow him, saying, "Tyler, come on son, it's time for two's and three's down the lane," I was pretty sure I knew what he meant!

The Lane Near our House

Dad told me that my new home used to be a farm, but that was many years ago. The old farm buildings had been converted into six houses, built around a little courtyard. Living on an old farm means there are lots of places to play, and there are no busy roads nearby that could easily cause a few problems for a puppy like me; in fact….. the 'road' outside our house quickly becomes a tractor path so I don't have to worry about passing cars. Dad still taught me the correct way to behave on the road though – he didn't want to take any chances with me!

The tractor path leads down to another farm and that is where I went with Dad for my daily walks. I can remember feeling very tired after my first ever walk – I didn't think my little legs would make it all the way home, but then I thought to myself – I should just soldier on without complaining and I'll soon get really fit if I do this every day!

The Biggest Dog in the World

As we got nearer to the house at the end of my first ever walk, I saw in the distance the beautiful girl with the happy, smiling face. I heard Dad shout out her name, and that was when I first discovered that she was called Sarah. She looked up and waved and called for me to come to her, and even though I was dog-tired, I was so excited that I mustered up enough energy to run towards her with my tail wagging like crazy. But just before I reached Sarah I had the biggest shock of my life – she had another dog, and was busy brushing his coat. He was absolutely massive - no, he was absolutely humongous!

I think my new Mum realised how shocked I was when I came to a skidding halt a few feet in front of her. She laughed really loudly and bent down to pick me up. Carrying me snugly in her arms she walked over to the scary-looking, gigantic dog and said, "Tyler – this is Monty." As we got close up to him, my ears flopped; my tail was wagging so slowly it had almost stopped, and my eyes were nearly completely shut as I nervously said, "Hello." Monty turned his huge head towards me, swished his tail, and I think he seemed to smile – well, I hoped it was a smile - he had such a lot of big white teeth that it was hard to tell!

When Sarah put me down I was very glad to be escaping the giant dog, so I ran towards the house and sped quickly over the sharp gravel on the driveway – 'ooh, ouch, ooh, ouch'! I was a lot happier when I saw the kitchen door was wide open, but in my haste I forgot about that slippery floor! This time, Tweedy the cat saw me coming and quickly got out of the way – "Hey Tweeds", I squeaked as I skidded right past her and bashed into the cupboards – "guess what - I'm going to be absolutely massive when I grow up – have you seen the size of the other dog that Sarah has outside?"

"Oh dear," said Tweedy, in a smug know-it-all sort of way. "You have got a lot to learn! You'll never be as big as that 'massive dog' – because he's not a dog, silly, he's a HORSE!"

I must admit, I did feel a bit silly, but I didn't dare ask Tweedy what a horse was and just decided to do my best to remember in future! I knew Tweedy was right – I was just a young puppy dog with a lot to learn, but Tweedy had lived with Sarah and my new Dad for a very long time, so she knew what was what. For some reason she was now a bad-tempered old cat who didn't think too much of me! I knew she liked her own space, and I could tell she didn't really want to be my friend, so I did my best to keep out of her way and made sure I didn't skid into her again – well – I tried not to!

Even though things hadn't started off too well with Tweedy, I had a funny feeling that I was going to be the best of friends with Monty.

Sarah can Ride!

Sarah woke up early on my second morning with my new family; her bedroom was above the kitchen where I slept and I think she must have heard me having a cry to myself in bed. She called upstairs to tell Dad and he said that perhaps I was a little home-sick, but just in case it was something more serious he asked my new Mum to telephone the doggy doctor, which you probably call a Vet.

I overheard Sarah telling the Vet that she was worried because I'd been whimpering away for quite a while, but when she explained about the long walk I'd had the day before, the Vet said he didn't need to see me because he was sure that my little legs were probably achy and sore after walking too much on my first day home.

He told Sarah that young puppies should only go on short walks to begin with so they can build up their strength, and he was certain that I'd just over-done things a little with all the excitement. Sarah promised that she'd be in charge of my walk for that day and would only take me for a little stroll into the lane, which I was quite glad about – that meant I'd be able to see Monty again!

Monty had his own house called a stable, which seemed very comfy and cosy. It was right next to our house, so he was never very far away. When it was time for Sarah to take me for a walk I followed her over to the stable. I was a little nervous as Sarah led Monty out – he was snorting away and swishing his tail, and I was wondering if he was going to be as nice to me as he had been the day before. I think he must have spotted me out of the corner of his eye because he suddenly stopped walking, bent down towards me, gave a little snort, and sniffed me so hard with his great big nose that I almost toppled over! Monty must have thought that was very funny because as he walked past he swished his tail again and smiled at me showing those enormous big white teeth!

I couldn't help thinking about yesterday when I'd thought Monty was a great big dog! I wondered to myself if perhaps Monty had thought I was a baby horse, especially as we both have the same colour hair! But then I thought, no – probably not – Monty is much cleverer than that!

Monty gets Fed

Sarah was about to give Monty his breakfast and he was getting very excited – his great big feet were dancing all over the place! His food bowl was so big - it looked just like a bucket - in fact, I think it was a bucket! Sarah told me to stand well back so I didn't get hurt because Monty wasn't used to me hanging around his feet – I was so small that she was afraid he might accidentally clip clop all over me!

Monty's food was completely different to mine, but he seemed to love every mouthful and made a lot of noise while munching away. Sarah was busy brushing his coat while he was eating and she was talking to me and explaining everything she was doing. I was learning such a lot, especially just how much hard work it is to keep Monty looking so nice.

A little while after Monty had finished breakfast Sarah put a funny-looking seat on his back, which she told me was called a saddle.

Then she put some straps around his head with reins attached. As Sarah was putting a special hat on her head, she called out, "Dad, we're ready", and as quick as a flash she climbed up onto Monty's back.

I must admit this sent me into a bit of a panic and I was worried that Sarah might fall off. But when Dad wandered over carrying a cup of tea, he didn't seem at all bothered about what Sarah was doing, so that made me feel a little better.

I sat quietly between Dad's feet to see what was going to happen next, and as Sarah gave the reins a little tug, off they went with a 'clip clop' – 'clip clop'. As they walked up the lane towards the top road I got all excited and started whimpering because I wanted to go with them, but Dad said, "Don't worry son, they'll be back very soon - it would be safer if we went for a little walk down the farmer's lane instead." As they turned the corner Sarah looked back and waved bye-bye to us both – Monty seemed to be waving too, and was excitedly swishing his tail from side to side.

Monty Loses a Shoe

While Sarah was out riding Monty, Dad decided to clean out the stable – I think it's called mucking out – whatever that means! I was busy getting in the way as usual, while doing my best not to get under Dad's feet, but as I had a sniff around, I thought to myself, "There's been no potty training going on in here!"

Dad worked very hard and in no time at all Monty's little house was nice and clean, with a fresh bed for him to lay on when it was time to go asleep. Just then my 'guard dog' ears heard Sarah and Monty coming home and I started jumping up and down with excitement. Dad was still working hard and I was trying to get his attention, but when he eventually realised why I was so excited, he sounded surprised and said, "They're back early."

As Sarah and Monty got closer and closer, the clip-clop became louder. Dad had a puzzled expression and thought something sounded different – the noise Monty was making with his feet was not the same as when they left. There was a clip-clip-CLOP – clip-clip-CLOP. "Oh dear," sighed Dad, "that sounds expensive." I didn't know what he meant, so I ran out into the lane and saw Sarah walking alongside Monty and carrying something shiny in her hand.

Sarah tied Monty to a big wooden post while she and Dad lifted his feet up one by one. Only three of his feet had shiny shoes on – two of those seemed loose, and Sarah had the fourth one in her hand. Dad said, "Oh well, they've lasted a bit longer than the last set of shoes – I'll call the Farrier."

I sort of guessed that a Farrier must be someone who puts new shoes on a horse, but then I started thinking to myself - a horse with shoes and no clothes? Sounds funny to me, but what do I know, I'm just a puppy dog!

New Shoes and a Trim

The Farrier happened to be in the area tending another horse when Dad telephoned, so he arrived very quickly. Monty seemed to love the fuss of having a new set of shoes put on, but it all seemed very noisy and confusing to me. There was lots of clatter, smelly smoke, and a very hot mini-furnace roaring away. The furnace was used to make the metal shoes red hot so they could be shaped to fit Monty's feet perfectly. This is done on what my Dad called an anvil, which is a sturdy piece of iron that is used to place the hot metal on while it's beaten into shape.

Everything was going very well, but all of a sudden I had a terrible fright and I just couldn't watch any more – I was scared stiff! I saw the Farrier take a hammer and nails out of his bag, and, believe it or not, he started to hammer the new shoes onto Monty's feet with real nails! Monty just looked over and seemed to be laughing at me, but I was horrified and couldn't stop yelping and running around in a panic! Monty has had plenty of shoes put on like this before, but I am just very glad that I'm a dog – I don't need any clothes and I definitely don't want any shoes!

When Dad could see how worried I was about what the Farrier was doing to Monty, he explained that horse hooves are similar to human finger and toe nails, but much tougher and thicker. He said the nails are used to hold the shoes in place and that a horse can't feel the Farrier hammering the nails into his hooves. Well, I kind of found that hard to believe, but Dad must be right – Monty wasn't at all upset and seemed to be enjoying all the attention!

Dad said it takes many years to learn how to become a Farrier, and takes lots of practice to become really good at the job. I think you have to be really brave as well – horse hooves need to be trimmed before each shoe can be fitted, so the job of a Farrier is a tricky one – imagine having to file a horse's hooves!

After the Farrier had gone, Sarah was just about to sweep up the mess when she had an idea and said, "Tyler, I think I'll show you something else new today – how would you like to see me trim some of Monty's long hair? If I don't do it soon Dad will have a go, and he's terrible with scissors – he can't cut a straight line for toffee!" Sarah told me that the last time Dad took a pair of scissors to Monty he trimmed his fringe, mane, fetlocks and tail – poor old Monty looked like a worn out teddy bear and it took ages for it all to grow back!

Horse hair is strong and tough and you need a special pair of scissors to cut it, so when she'd finished and swept up all the mess, Sarah decided it would be a good idea to hide the scissors so Dad wouldn't be tempted to 'have another go'. I had a good look at those scissors and remembered exactly where Sarah had put them – if I ever saw Dad heading in my direction armed with those special scissors, I'd make a run for it – I didn't want to end up looking like a worn out teddy bear!

Part 2: Monty and Me

Sarah leaves Home

A special letter was delivered this week for Sarah – she was very keen to become a soldier in the Army and had been invited to go and stay with them for a few days. The letter included a list of all the things she needed to take and told her about everything she'd be doing during her stay, but I didn't really understand what was happening. When I heard her say she was going upstairs to pack her bags I became quite upset – I thought that perhaps she'd finally been sold, just like me!

Tweedy was nowhere to be seen so I couldn't ask her what was going on, and Sarah was busy in her bedroom with the door closed tight, so I curled up on the floor outside her room and started to have a little cry to myself. Sarah must have overheard me whimpering and came outside. She picked me up and gave me a great big cuddle. Somehow, she seemed to know why I was crying and said, "Oh Tyler, don't get upset – I'm not leaving forever, I'll be back in a few days." Oh gosh, was I pleased to hear that! I wagged my tail as fast as I could and gave her lots of sloppy kisses, which made her laugh really loud.

Once Sarah was sure I was happy again, she put me down, but then she called out to Dad saying, "Dad, I'm going to need a favour in the morning – could you give me a lift to the station – is that okay?"

"No problem," Dad called back.

For a moment I felt a little sad again, but I kept telling myself not to be so silly. As it turned out, this was not the first time Sarah had made a journey to visit the Army. Dad seemed to be used to dropping her off at the main railway station in Carlisle, but I wasn't at all happy to be saying goodbye – not one little bit.

When it came time for Sarah to leave, I wasn't in the best of moods. Even though I knew she had promised to come home soon, I was still very upset inside. Dad carried Sarah's heavy suitcase downstairs and put it in the car while Sarah went to the stable to say goodbye to Monty. I've never really got over that feeling of sadness, and whenever I see a suitcase it reminds me of Sarah saying goodbye, and my little eyes well up with tears. Except, of course, if we're all going on holiday and I can see my bag being packed as well – THAT'S different!

While Dad and Sarah were loading everything into the car, I was standing around feeling really miserable and waiting patiently for my goodbye hug. I tried my best to keep wagging my tail, but it wasn't easy. Just then, Sarah looked down at me and called out to Dad saying, "Could Tyler come to the station with us?"

"Well, alright, but only if you put plenty of newspaper in the car for him to stand on 'just in case' – if you know what I mean," replied Dad.

To my delight Sarah scooped me up, gave me a great big cuddle and a kiss, and put me down on a nice little newspaper-bed in the back of the car! My tail wasn't having any trouble wagging now!

The journey to the station only took about 20 minutes and when we arrived Dad parked the car and jumped out, but I did have a bit of a fright. The hatchback door flew open ever so quickly, which made me jump, but then Sarah appeared and leaned inside the car to say goodbye. It reminded me of the day I saw her face for the very first time as my kennel door opened and she reached inside and picked me up. Even though she'd promised she would be back soon, I couldn't stop the little tears from rolling down my face as she gave me her final wave before closing the door again. I stretched up as high as I could and watched through the car window as Dad walked with Sarah to the train platform carrying her case. I tried my very best to be a grown up dog and not cry too much, but it wasn't easy - I was still a little puppy dog.

Dad waited with Sarah until she'd boarded the train and it had left the station, but when he came back to the car I could see he'd been crying too – he was all puffy eyed and sniffling. Even though he stroked my head and reassured me by saying he had a bit of a cold, I knew better.

The journey home was very quiet, and when we arrived the house felt so empty – we both knew it wouldn't be the same until Sarah was home again.

Monty misses Sarah

Once Dad had made himself a cup of tea and was feeling a little better after his goodbyes at the station, he realised it was time for Monty's daily exercise, but there was one small problem - Dad hadn't ridden a horse since he was a young pup... er, I mean, a young boy, so Monty's 'exercise' was never quite the same when Sarah was away!

Dad decided that he was going to take me for a walk at the same time as Monty – a real adventure for me and not something I'd done before. When we got to the stable Dad put a lead rope around Monty's neck and off we went down the lane and into the farmer's field. I could tell Monty wasn't too impressed because every now and then he'd let out a few very loud snorts, shake his head, and do a little clip-clop dance while looking over at Dad as if to say, "What kind of exercise do you call this?"

Over the next few days we followed the same routine, but even I could see that Monty was becoming more and more fed up – he was missing Sarah as much as we were, but he was also missing galloping through the fields and their rides along the top road. Monty's snorts became louder than ever, and his clip-clop dance made it very clear that he was quite annoyed by only having a feeble 'dog walk' instead of being taken out by a proper rider.

After a few days of Monty's moodiness, Dad became quite tired of it all, so he suddenly looked Monty straight in the eyes and said, "Okay, I give in... but if I ride you, we walk, we just walk – nothing fast and definitely no fancy foot-work from you – okay Monty – do you promise?"

Monty nodded his head and swished his tail as if to say, "I promise – well, sort of!" He had a twinkle in his eyes and he glanced down at me as if to say, "Whatever!"

It was so funny watching Dad trying to remember how to put a saddle and reins on Monty – he tried one way then another – I did my best not to laugh, but Monty wasn't able to control himself! His fed-up snorts had now turned into a toothy hee-haw grin as he swung his head around from side to side to check if Dad had got it right yet!

Dad didn't have any proper riding gear so he made do with a pair of muddy wellington boots and an old riding hat from the stable. He did look a bit of a sight, but he didn't care – he was only going to ride down our little lane and no one would see him.

Before setting off for his very first ride on Monty, Dad scooped me up and took me to my bed in the kitchen, quickly closing the door behind him. For the first time ever I was all alone in a big, empty house, and I panicked. I cried and cried so loud that Dad came straight back and tried to explain why I couldn't go with him. He was worried about riding Monty on his own and said he couldn't look after me at the same time. I tried to understand, but I still wasn't happy. Dad stroked my head and said he'd be back soon and closed the door behind him again, but I couldn't help it.... I cried and cried even louder. Once more, Dad came back into the kitchen and said, "I'm not going to be able to do this am I Tyler – you'll be in a right old state if I leave you here on your own.

" Phew, that's a relief," I thought to myself!

My First Ride on a Horse

Before Dad could change his mind, I scooted through the open door and ran out in front of him towards the stable. I could see Monty had a disapproving look on his face because he'd been kept waiting, but little did he know what was going to happen next! A few seconds later Dad appeared at the stable door and began taking off his riding hat while saying to Monty, "Sorry son, we can't leave Tyler on his own in the house in such a state." Well, if you'd have heard Monty's reaction! The clip-clop dance became more like a war-dance, and Monty's snorts of disapproval were directed straight at me. I was cowering a little because I did feel a bit guilty, and I could tell Dad felt bad too. Then, just as Dad was about to take Monty's saddle off I could tell he'd had an idea – he started thinking aloud and was saying, "I wonder – I wonder...."

Monty and I could tell that something was ticking over in Dad's mind, so we both stood quietly and waited while he disappeared for a moment. He returned with some strong wooden boxes that he piled on top of one another next to the stable door. Then Dad picked me up in his arms, climbed on top of the boxes, and somehow managed to wriggle his way onto Monty's back and settle us both down in the saddle.

Well, this was the last thing we thought he'd do! Monty gave me a real 'funny look' as he stretched his head as far back as he could to try and see what was going on, and find out exactly 'who or what' had just got on his back!

At that time I was small enough to fit inside Dad's coat and was able to pop my head out after he'd unfastened a few buttons, so I felt quite safe up there. And as for Monty – well, he got over it pretty quickly! His ears began to twitch and he gave a great big shiver, did a little dance to test out his brand new shoes, then gently turned and began to walk slowly down the lane.

Dad was a little nervous at first and so was I - this was my first ride on a horse and his first ride for a very long time, and I can tell you.... it certainly took some getting used to! Being so high up off the ground didn't feel too great in the beginning, and the strange, jerky movements Monty made when he walked had me wondering why on earth people actually do this! In fact, I'm sure I overheard Dad muttering away to himself and saying exactly the same thing!

All of this was a lot for a puppy dog to take in, but with a bit of practice and a lot of patience from Dad, I began to love every minute of it. I don't think it was long before Monty started enjoying it as well – he started to huff and puff quite proudly – I think he thought he was the bees-knees as he was probably the only horse in the whole world to be taking a puppy dog for a ride!

I didn't mind Monty feeling proud because he'd made me feel really special. High up on his back I could now see what he could see – rather than just sniffing around on the ground like normal puppy dogs do, I could see for miles and miles, and the best part of all – my little legs weren't so sore when we got back home because now I didn't have to do all the walking!

Going Solo

There was one very special day that I'll always remember. It had begun just like any other day, but it turned out to be anything but! We'd arrived home from our daily ride, and as usual I was getting myself into all sorts of trouble by scampering around Monty's feet while Dad was taking off the saddle. As Dad was telling me to come out from under Monty in case I got hurt, he noticed that Monty's shoes seemed to have a lot of mud stuck to them. He knew that small stones could get jammed in the mud, making it very uncomfortable or even painful for him to walk, so this had to be sorted out straight away. Monty seemed pleased that Dad had noticed his shoes were a little clogged up and he was probably grateful that this pesky puppy dog had drawn Dad's attention to the problem!

Because Monty was such a grown-up, clever horse he knew exactly what to do when it was time to have his shoes unclogged, and each time Dad put his hand near one of Monty's feet, he automatically bent his leg upwards so Dad could clean his shoe with a special tool called a hoof pick. I thought this was very interesting so I wandered over to have a closer look. Monty wasn't happy to see me under his feet, and because a horse can sometimes lose its balance when this is being done, Dad shouted at me to get out from underneath Monty! But I was a little naughty and couldn't resist snooping around! In the end Dad became frustrated – he suddenly jumped to his feet, scooped me up in the air, and, without thinking, plonked me straight onto Monty's back!

Well, Monty was stunned – but Monty being such a clever horse he probably quickly decided that having his feet sorted out was more important than tossing me off his back – I suppose he thought that could wait a few minutes! But for me, this was just the greatest thing in the world EVER! I wasn't going to do anything to upset Monty or Dad because I didn't want to be told off and have to get down, so I just sat there patiently watching Monty's ears twitching and I didn't say a puppy-word!

Because I'd been riding with Dad almost every day I was used to being high off the ground, but Dad thought it was amazing that I didn't want to get down or that Monty wasn't frightened or upset because a dog was sitting on his bare back! Most horses don't like dogs to be anywhere near them, and certainly not sitting on top of them! Dad carried on 'picking out' all of Monty's feet and chatted away to the two of us to keep us both calm. But what none of us would have guessed at the time was that this was the start of something very big – I don't think Dad had any idea what he'd just done!

When Dad had finished with Monty's feet he looked up at the two of us and was in fits of giggles – what a sight we must have been! We both looked back at him as if to say, "What's so funny?" Dad must have been in the mood for a little experimenting, because he slowly untied Monty's lead rope and began walking us both a short distance across the lane and back. He was a little anxious though; it was a long way down for a little puppy and he thought that at any moment either I'd become scared and jump for it, or Monty would throw me off, but that didn't happen. I was as good as gold and having the time of my life, and I could sense that Monty was too. Dad said later that Monty had the biggest toothy grin on his face that he'd ever seen!

I'd been on so many horse rides with Dad that I was used to the movement Monty makes when he walks, and it didn't really seem any different except that this time nobody was holding on to me and I wasn't peeking out of the top of Dad's jacket! But Dad kept a careful eye on the two of us and chatted away to keep us calm as we walked up and down the lane. I could tell that Monty was proud of me for staying on his back without falling off, and Dad kept telling me what a good job I was doing, but because I'd been riding lots of times before, I didn't think I'd done anything special – I was just very excited that I'd had my very first ride on a horse without any help from anyone, and I couldn't wait to run inside to tell Tweedy!

Water Everywhere!

"What a night," said Dad, "it hasn't rained like that for as long as I can remember, but at least it's stopped now." He was right – we'd been kept awake most of the night with rain lashing down, and as Dad looked out of the kitchen window, he said, "I think we should skip riding Monty this morning and we'll just go for a walk on our own today Tyler. It's going to be too muddy and slippery for Monty and we don't want him getting into trouble or hurting himself."

This was a nice change for me – I don't feel like I'm a puppy now, and I like having a good run around, especially when Dad throws a ball for me. My legs seem stronger than ever and I don't get tired or feel sore after a long walk, and when we're on our own I can do some serious exploring and have a good sniff of everything around and about. For dogs, all the different smells tell us quite a lot – it's a bit like smelly-vision instead of television!

Once the rain had completely stopped, Dad and I headed towards the farmer's fields at the bottom of the lane. When we arrived, that's when we realised just how much rain had fallen during the night – the fields were so flooded that we could hardly see the ground or the paths! This was the first time I'd seen rain water like this and I was so excited – I wanted to explore and have some 'puppy' fun splashing in the puddles! Fortunately,

35

Dad didn't seem to mind me getting soaking wet, and told me that all Labradors love water and become very good swimmers when they're older, so I didn't need any more encouragement than that – as soon as I had the chance I was going to test out my water wings!

We walked a little bit further while trying to stay on the path, but then Dad suddenly realised that I was wandering too far away from him. He started to shout in a panicky sort of way, "Tyler come away from there, be careful – there's a great big ditch right in front of you and it's very deep."

Well, I heard Dad calling out to me but I didn't know what a ditch was! Besides, the water was so muddy that I couldn't see a thing – all I could think about was how much fun I was having jumping in and out of millions of puddles!

Tyler Gets a Fright

The 'ditch' that Dad was so worried about was full of muddy water, but to me it looked the same as all the fields I'd been splashing around in, so I had no idea that it wasn't 'just another little puddle' but a great big deep one full of fast-flowing flood water!

Dad shouted again, but this time he was yelling at me, "Tyler come away from there," but it was too late. With just one more step I was in the ditch – head first, with a splutter and a gulp, I went right under! All I can remember was how cold and deep it was - I couldn't see a thing because of the force of the water, which was muddy and moving very fast. I was tumbling over and over and being whisked away. My little legs were kicking as hard as they could, but the current was too strong – I couldn't do anything to stop and was disappearing further and further downstream.

By now, Dad wouldn't have been able to see me at all and must have been in a right old state – I'd completely disappeared under water – no matter how hard he looked, he wouldn't have been able to see any sign of me.

But good old Dad immediately put his quick-thinking hat on. He tried to guess where I was most likely to reappear out of the rushing water, and as quick as a flash he chased off in that direction. As luck would have it, Dad's guess was right!

My head popped up almost exactly where Dad thought it would, but he was still racing across muddy fields trying to reach me. I looked around desperately while gasping for air, but I couldn't see him anywhere. I took a big, deep breath of fresh air and squealed as loud as I could, "Dad, Dad - help – Dad," but I still couldn't see him! Then I felt as though I was being pulled back under the water again, so I started to panic. I hadn't learned to swim yet, so my little paws just splashed and splashed. But by now I was so cold and weak that it didn't do any good. I had just about enough energy left to take another big, deep breath and shout for Dad one last time as the rushing water began to pull me under again. Then, all of a sudden, I felt Dad's strong hand grab my collar, and haul me through the air and out of the muddy mess!

I wasn't hurt but I'd had such a big shock. I was shivering and scared - I just cried and cried. Although I was covered in mud, that didn't matter to Dad. He just picked me up and wrapped his coat around me because I was freezing cold, soaking wet, and still crying my little heart out! He did his best to keep me warm by cuddling me very tight and rushed me home as quickly as he could.

I could tell Dad was exhausted when we got home, and was almost as wet and muddy as I was! And as for his coat – well, I think that was the end of that! Just then, Tweedy wandered into the kitchen and when Dad told her what a lucky escape I'd had, she smugly walked away while mumbling to herself, "Maybe next time you take that dog for a walk you should make him wear a lifejacket!" Well, I didn't think that was very funny at all!

Once Dad had dried us both off, he said, "Tyler you've just given me the biggest fright of my life young man – please don't EVER do that again! I think I'll take you upstairs and give you a bath to clean you properly and warm you up."

I was a little confused – "What on earth is a 'bath'," I said to myself. I quickly looked around for Tweedy, and in a bit of a panic I shouted, "Tweedy, Tweedy – what is a bath – is it going to hurt?"

She smirked sneakily at me, and meowed to herself while curling up in her nice warm bed, and said, "You're just about to find out my mucky little friend. You're just about to find out!"

"Huh," I thought to myself, "that cat is really getting on my nerves now!"

Heart-to-heart

The following morning I was still feeling a little tired because I hadn't slept very well. I kept waking up with a fright and remembering how I'd fallen into the ditch and been swept downstream. Just as I was looking around and checking to see if there was any breakfast in my bowl, Dad opened the door and Tweedy sauntered in for a drink of water. While giving me one of her usual sideways looks, she told me that Monty had been asking if I was okay, so I decided to dash over to see him.

As I bounded towards Monty's stable he whinnied loudly as he heard me coming and said, "Goodness me Tyler, it sounds as though you had a lucky escape."

Well, Monty was right – I knew I'd been very lucky, so I sheepishly replied, "Yes, I did, but it was thanks to Dad – he saved my life – he was very clever and very brave."

It turned out that Monty not only knew what had happened, but also knew a little more detail: "Tweedy told me all about it," replied Monty, "and she said that when Dad pulled you out of the water, he nearly fell in too!"

Well, that was a shock – I hadn't realised that Dad was in danger as well, but I'd been so cold and wet that I didn't really know what was going on. At least now I understood why Dad had seemed as muddy and wet as me!

Just then Dad came over to the stable to give Monty an apple, so I ran to him wagging my tail as fast as I could. I weaved myself tightly in and out of his legs, which was my little way of saying an extra big thank you for saving me from that muddy mess. Dad looked down at me, picked me up, and gave me a big cuddle. Then Monty popped his very large head over the stable door and had a great big sniff of me with his huge nose. I suppose that was the nearest thing to a kiss that a puppy dog was ever going to get from a horse!

Getting Better at Riding

Almost every day until Sarah returned home, Dad and I would ride out on Monty, but before we put Monty back in his stable Dad would take off the saddle and put me on Monty's back, then we'd walk up and down the lane going a little further each day. I was becoming so good at riding that even if Monty tripped or stumbled on some rough ground, I would still be able to keep my balance.

Occasionally I did fall off, but sometimes I'd jump off if I got over-excited and saw a rabbit or something I could chase! Dad didn't like it when I did that because he felt he was now training me to ride properly, and my 'jumping off' stunt was counted as being naughty, especially when we started going a little faster and further each day, and even more especially now that we were walking along The Top Road!

The day finally arrived when Sarah was due home from her visit to the Army. She'd had a really good time and had lots of news to tell us. We'd missed her a lot, but I tried hard not to show how much fun we'd all secretly been having! I couldn't wait to let her see how good I was at riding Monty all on my own – she was going to be so amazed!

Dad told Sarah that I'd learned a brand new trick and that we were going to give her a demonstration - I think Sarah probably thought I'd learned some 'really useful' puppy trick like chasing a ball – imagine that! I could tell that Dad was just as excited as I was to show Sarah what we'd been up to, so the morning after she'd arrived home we went out to the stable to see Monty. Dad put a lead rope on Monty and brought him out of his stable so he could see Sarah properly, then, in the blink of an eye, Dad suddenly picked me up and put me on Monty's back, he threw the lead rope over Monty's neck, and we walked into the lane by ourselves.

Sarah was astounded and thought it was the funniest thing she'd ever seen – she was laughing so much that I thought she was going to cry! "That's absolutely fantastic," she said, "I knew you'd be a clever dog when we got you Tyler, but I didn't imagine you'd be this clever!" I was now so in the good books and was grinning from ear to ear! Sarah said, "Look Dad, Tyler is actually smiling" - which turned out to be another unusual trick I could do!

While Sarah was home she had lots of work to do in preparation for her new job in the Army, so she was too busy to ride out on Monty every day. But that was okay with us! Dad didn't mind exercising Monty now; in fact, he was really enjoying riding again and was getting better and better each day. Whenever I saw him put his wellington boots on, I knew it was time to race out to the stables and tell Monty we were going riding again. But the really good thing about all of this was discovering that Dad is a bit of a dare-devil on the quiet! Each time it was my turn to ride Monty, he let me go faster and faster and further and further. I didn't know it then, but in a few weeks time I would be good enough to ride Monty even if he started to run! How about that!

In Trouble with the Police

By now lots of people had either seen or heard about me riding Monty along the top road, and every day more and more people on bicycles or in cars would slow down or stop to get a closer look. Anyone who had a camera asked if they could take a picture, and if they didn't have a camera with them, they'd come back with one the next day. Sometimes there were so many people stopping that we had our own private traffic jam, but nobody seemed to mind because they'd all come to see me riding on Monty's back.

What Dad hadn't realised was that Monty was camera-shy and hated having his picture taken, so he wouldn't stand still when people tried to take a photograph. Quite often he actually misbehaved on purpose by dancing around and swishing his tail until they stopped clicking their camera and went away!

One day, when there were a few cars slowing down to watch, Dad noticed a police car at the back of the queue, so it wasn't long before all the other cars moved on. The police car drove past us very slowly with one of the officers looking up at me and scratching his head. Then the car pulled over a little further along the road by the farmer's gate and two policemen got out. That's when we all thought, "Uh oh – we're in trouble now!" We needn't have worried though – one of the policemen had a camera and he only wanted to take a picture of us! "Phew," I thought, "that was a close shave with the law!"

Dad thought it was best to keep moving along even though the policemen were walking towards us, but as soon as one of the officers pointed a camera in our direction, Dad realised Monty was having none of it! "Oh no – don't you dare start anything now," said Dad as Monty began his little 'dance' to make the policemen go away!

While Dad was doing his best to calm Monty down, one of police officers said, "Could I have a word sir?"

"Certainly – there's nothing wrong is there?" asked Dad.

"No," said the policeman, who started to giggle, "but shouldn't your dog be wearing a 'high viz' jacket when he's out riding?"

Everyone burst out laughing as they imagined how funny a dog would look wearing a brightly coloured 'high visibility' jacket while sitting on top of a horse! VERY funny I thought to myself! But Dad being Dad – that little joke got him thinking, so later that afternoon he got to work in his shed!

When Sarah was a little girl and was allowed to go riding on the top road, she had to wear a brightly coloured jacket so motorists could see her from a long way off. Her jacket had some writing on the back of it that said, 'Please pass wide and slow.' The jacket was far too small for her now, but with the help of those sharp horse-hair scissors that Sarah was supposed to have hidden, Dad made a few 'expert' alterations with a snip here and a bit of stitching there, and before I knew it, Sarah's old jacket fitted me perfectly. Every day from then on, I had to wear my 'high viz' jacket, much to everyone's amusement! But more especially, just in case those policemen came back!

Part 3: Now we are Famous

Trust and Friendship

The sight of Monty and me riding along The Top Road eventually became an everyday occurrence for people living in our village, but a stranger must have thought it was quite a special sight to see because it wasn't long before someone told the local newspaper about us! A reporter telephoned Dad and asked if he could come to our house and take some photographs and do a little story on Monty and me. Dad explained that Monty was really very camera-shy and might not stand still for the photographer, but the man from the newspaper wasn't worried about that. He said the cameraman was used to photographing at horse shows so it wouldn't be a problem. Dad agreed while having a bit of a laugh to himself, saying, "But don't say I didn't warn you!"

The people from the newspaper were due to arrive mid-morning on the following day, so Dad busied himself preparing us both for our first official photo-shoot, and I did my very best not to get in his way. Even Tweedy became a little interested in why there was so much activity, and ventured over to the stable to satisfy her curiosity! For ages she'd done her best to pretend she wasn't at all interested in my new riding skill, but I think she must have overheard Dad talking on the phone and wanted to make sure she wasn't left out of all the fame that was about to come our way!

I didn't mind Tweedy hanging around, but I didn't want it to seem as though I was showing off – I just wanted her to see that I wasn't the silly little puppy she thought I was! But Tweedy had never seen Monty do his little dance before, so I didn't expect it would be long before she'd get a big fright and run off! The moment a camera was pointed in Monty's direction, I knew he'd 'start' and we'd not see Tweedy for dust!

While Dad was working hard grooming us so we'd look our best, he was chatting away and telling us about all of the things we had to do before the newspaper men arrived, and that's when something he said got me thinking. "Don't forget there are two stars in this show Tyler, and you both have to look smart and clean."

All the while I'd been thinking that this was just about me and that I was the clever one who could ride a horse. I thought it was just me that the newspaper reporters were coming to see, but then it dawned on me – I'd not thought this whole thing through at all. You see, if Monty had not wanted me up there on his back and learning to ride, he could easily have put a stop to it and flung me off by doing a lot more than just a little dance! That was when I began to understand something very important. It was our friendship and how we trusted one another that were the special things – this wasn't just about a dog doing a clever trick.

I realised then that it was Monty who'd allowed me to ride on his back all this time, and together we were a great team. This whole thing isn't about me at all – it's about a loving and trusting relationship between a dog, a horse, and Dad, our owner, and, of course, that funny old cat Tweedy! I love her too – really, I do!

The Photo Shoot

Well, Dad was right - and so was I – Monty did his best dance EVER as soon as he saw the newspaper cameraman moving towards the stable! And the other thing I was right about was Tweedy – the moment Monty began his little dance, that old cat ran faster than I've ever seen a cat run in my life! I chuckled so much that Dad thought I was choking on something!

The camera was quite big compared to what people use on the top road. It made a very loud clicking noise and had lots of flashing lights, which upset Monty even more than usual – he didn't just do a little dance, but gave a few good snorts as well! Dad decided it would be best if we went down the lane to the farmer's field to take the photographs, and because Monty was clearly not going to stand for any nonsense from a 'giant' camera, Dad also suggested that the man hide in the bushes and use a big long-distance lens to get his photos.

Dad and I thought that would make things easier, but Monty is very clever. No matter how much we tried to pretend that no one was hiding, Monty knew better! He kept a very close eye on those bushes at all times, and kept sending a great big angry snort in that direction to make sure the cameraman knew Monty could still see him!

Eventually I think Monty sort of liked the idea that the man was having to go to so much trouble to get his photos, so as long as he didn't come anywhere near him, he thought he'd do a bit of strutting about just for fun! Huh! It might have been fun for him, but I had a real hard time just trying to stay on his back!

By the time we came back up the lane Monty had almost become used to the cameraman and was beginning to enjoy being a star. Of course, it could have been the sight of the poor cameraman covered in mud and his dirty jacket that made Monty so happy, but for whatever reason he'd stopped making a fuss, which meant we were able to get some great shots of Monty and me riding along the top road.

Even though Monty had been a little bit naughty, Dad told us that the pictures had turned out really well and the newspaper had said some very nice things about us. In fact, the article was so popular in our local newspaper that the big city newspapers asked if they could use them. So, not only were we famous in our own town, but now we were famous all over the country!

We'd had lots of fun doing the photo-shoot and our family and friends had really enjoyed seeing us in the newspapers. But just as Dad was cutting out the articles and saying we should make a scrapbook to keep them in, the phone rang and we had some surprising news.

I was sitting waiting patiently looking up at Dad and was a little confused about what he was saying, but when he put the phone down he turned to me and said, "I don't believe it Tyler – guess what - that was the television people – they want to come and film us for a local television news programme!"

As Dad went into the kitchen to make a cup of tea, I overheard him saying to himself that if poor old Monty was upset about the size of the newspaper man's camera, what on earth was going to happen when a great big monster TV camera was staring him straight in the face!

We are on TV!

It didn't seem long after the phone call before the television people were knocking on our front door. There were two men – one was carrying a great big hairy microphone and the other had the biggest camera I'd ever seen! They arrived so quickly that Dad didn't have much time to get us ready, so he thought we'd just have to get on with it and hope for the best.

The television men had lots of questions to ask before filming started, but once everyone was ready they wondered if it would be okay if we all went up to the top road to do the filming.

Dad wasn't so sure about that because he'd not had time to have a chat with Monty and let him know what was going to happen, so he suggested we have a little practice in the lane first to see how Monty behaves.

Well, Monty was true to form and 'behaved' as we expected – dancing and prancing all over the place, snorting at the camera, and swishing his tail like crazy! "Oh dear," said Dad as he looked down at me with a sigh, "I think this is going to be a very long day Tyler!"

The television cameramen asked Dad if he could try to calm Monty down, so he took some apples over to Monty and had a little chat in his ear to reassure him. But it didn't really work – it wasn't the filming that upset him, just the size of the huge camera that was following him around everywhere! Poor Monty – I did feel sorry for him. Dad quickly realised that he wasn't just camera-shy – he was really frightened, and I wasn't too happy either – by now we weren't so sure that this was really such a good idea any more.

Monty was so nervous that he kept forgetting that I was on his back, and even though Dad had tight hold of his lead rope to steady him, I fell off quite a few times! Eventually I decided that perhaps I too should have a little whisper in Monty's ear, and that's when I reminded him that if he behaved himself we'd be even more famous – now we'd be television stars and not just newspaper stars!

I could see Monty's ears twitch a little as he was giving this some serious thought, and I think it helped. Even though it took ages to get the filming right, and we had to practice over and over again – take 1...take 2 ...take 3.....take 325 – we did get it right in the end, and I was relieved when I heard the cameraman shout in TV language, "Cut – that's a wrap!"

After they left we were all very tired, so Dad took Monty back to his stable where he could have a well-earned rest. He gave Monty some extra apples and carrots as a reward for getting it right in the end, and then he said to me, "Come on Tyler, let's go inside, make a nice cup of tea and have our dinner, then we can see if we've made the 'big time' on tonight's television."

Yes, it had been a long, hard day for us all, and after my extra special meal I cuddled up next to Dad on the couch and was almost fast asleep. But I was soon wide awake again when Dad suddenly shouted, "There we are Tyler – we're on television!" It was really exciting to see Monty and me on TV, but in the blink of an eye it was all over! "I don't believe it," said Dad, "it took hours to do all that filming but we were only on television for a few minutes!"

I thought to myself, "Well never mind – what they did show on television was great and I'd really enjoyed the whole day." But the following morning, just as we were thinking that our TV fame was over and our lives would begin to return to normal, the phone rang again.

In the same way that the local newspaper story had been picked up by the big national newspapers, the local TV station's film had caught the attention of the big national television stations. Lots of other TV people thought it was a great story to tell and they wanted to come from all over the country to film us!

When Dad put the phone down he walked over to me while shaking his head and laughing to himself and said, "Guess what Tyler – you two chaps have really hit the big time – now you're going to be on NATIONAL television!" Hollywood here we come!

A New Bond with Tweedy

It wasn't only lots of TV people that phoned Dad, but in the end all sorts of different newspapers and magazines wanted to take pictures and write stories about us – it went on and on for ages, and even though it was great fun, we were all exhausted when it was over.

For all of the hard work we'd done, the newspapers and magazines had made quite a bit of money out of our little story, but we didn't get anything - not even a tin of dog food for me or an apple for Monty! Perhaps Dad should have hired an agent!

Sarah phoned later that day to say she would be home again soon and that all of her Army friends had been watching us on television. They couldn't believe that the super-clever pets on the TV and in the newspapers all lived at her house! It was a pity Sarah hadn't been home when this all happened – she'd have probably thought about asking the television and newspaper people to make a donation to an animal charity in exchange for the photos and the hours and hours of time we gave to do their filming, but never mind – the opportunity was gone, or so we thought!

The next day everything had gone quiet – there were no phone calls or visitors and life was back to normal, and that was when Dad had an idea. I was sitting outside Monty's stable when he walked over carrying Tweedy. He sat down next to me and said he had a plan. "Tyler," he said, "now that you and Monty are so famous, what do you think about using that fame to raise some money for Tweedy's old home, the animal rescue centre? We could do a sponsored walk and we could do it with lots of other people and their pets too."

I didn't really know what a sponsored walk was, but I found out later that people sign a form to say they'll donate a certain amount of money to charity if someone promises to do something like a long walk or a run. Dad said, "Tyler, if you were to lead the walk on Monty's back and we asked lots of other people with pets to join in behind us, we could make a lot of money for the animal rescue shelter." I jumped up and did a good old-fashioned tail-wagging session, and that was how Dad knew I thought it was a good idea too! But first of all, Dad had to check with the rescue shelter to make sure they'd be happy for us to do this.

Dad put Tweedy down next to me while he went to make the phone call, so I asked her, "What's does Dad mean when he says 'your old home' Tweedy?" – and that was when she told me her story.

Tweedy didn't have a family to go to when she was a kitten and she had to live in a rescue shelter for unwanted pets. She told me what it was like to have to live in a place like that, and I must admit that I felt a little sorry for poor old Tweedy. She said that although the people who looked after the pets were really nice, they were always running short of money for food and any medicine the animals needed.

Now I understood why Dad wanted to raise some money and use our new-found fame to help out, but I was curious about how Tweedy ended up living here with Dad, Sarah and Monty, so I asked her how that happened.

I thought Tweedy might not be too keen to talk, but as it turned out she was quite excited that I'd asked, and said, "The same as you, Tyler. Do you remember the day you became part of our family? You told me that one morning your kennel door opened and you saw Sarah standing there and you thought she was the prettiest girl you'd ever seen."

I was a little confused at first, but said, "Yes, of course I remember."

As Tweedy began to strut around looking a little self-important, she then explained, "Well, the same thing happened to me. I was chosen by Sarah in the same way she chose you! We were both especially chosen....what do you think of that Tyler?"

I remember feeling quite shocked at first, but then I yelped with delight – this was so exciting – Sarah had chosen me as a puppy and also chosen Tweedy as a kitten! From that moment on I knew I had a very special friend with an even more special bond – a cat named Tweedy!

Fundraising Fame

When Dad returned from making his phone call he was very pleased – he said the people at the animal rescue shelter were delighted with the idea of a sponsored walk. They said they'd help us advertise it by asking everyone they knew if they'd be kind enough to join in. The only special thing we had to do was put the name of the rescue shelter on proper sponsorship forms to make sure we'd be able to collect all the money from those who'd donated.

Dad thought it would be a good idea if the forms had a picture of me riding Monty on the top, and that plan worked a treat because it encouraged lots and lots of people to come with their children and pets; not only to take part in the sponsored walk, but also because they wanted to see me riding Monty!

Even though the weather forecast for the day of the walk was for very heavy rain, it turned out to be a red-hot summer day! Lots of people enjoyed seeing us leading the sponsored walk around the countryside, and were very generous when they discovered it was for such a good cause. People recognised Monty and me from the television and newspapers, and they were very excited to see us in real life.

Because it was such a hot day, the walk was thirsty-work for everyone, so when we arrived back at the starting point all of the pets were given some water to drink and Dad and the other grown-ups had cups of tea. The children had a special treat and were given an ice cream each. Monty wasn't left out of the treats, and was rewarded with a couple of nice big juicy apples. He was worn out at the end of the walk because so many children and their pets were rushing around his feet and he was quite worried in case he stood on one of them. But Monty did really well and was very careful – Dad and I had told him the event was for an animal charity so he wanted to do his bit and he didn't play up at all, even though lots of cameras were pointing at us all day long!

The grown-ups counted the money we'd raised and Dad said it was fantastic because we'd made a whole heap of money for the homeless animals. And as a little surprise, all of the children were going to receive a personal letter in the post later that week because the rescue shelter was going to send a very special thank you to them all.

As everybody was saying goodbye, dark clouds started to gather in the sky. Dad said we'd better hurry-up and get home because it looked as though it was going to rain after all.

We were very lucky to finish the walk before the weather turned nasty, but now we had to rush and quickly get Monty back to his stable.

As with everything else that day we were very lucky and arrived back home just as some great big plip-plops of rain started to fall. We were all glad to be back, but Monty wasn't so happy when the thunder started, and neither was I for that matter! This was my very first thunder storm and I had no idea what was happening!

I felt sorry for Monty because he had to stay by himself in the stable, but I was able to cuddle up with my newest best friend – old Tweedy cat! We hid behind the sofa until the noisy thunder storm was over!

Sarah's Big Surprise

A few days later, I was curled up lying in the sun having a snooze by the stable and Dad was busy grooming Monty, when suddenly I heard a car pull into our driveway. I decided I should do what a guard dog does best, and I hid behind Dad's legs!

I started barking quite loudly while pretending to be a lot bigger than I am, but just as Dad began heading towards the front of the stable we heard another dog loudly barking back at me! Now I was a little worried – I looked up at Dad who was just as confused. I started to think that maybe I shouldn't have barked quite so loudly and that perhaps it might be a good idea if Dad picked me up – like, right now! I tried to scamper up his legs but it was no use – he was busy wondering who on earth our unexpected visitor could be!

But before he took another step Sarah came rushing into the garden and shouted, "Surprise – I'm home." Dad was so happy to see her smiling face – she'd been away with the Army yet again and he was so glad she was home safe and sound. I started yapping and wagging my tail like mad while running around looking for a ball or a stick to fetch. Dad was grinning from ear to ear as he opened up his arms and gave Sarah a great big hug. But just then, we had another big surprise – we suddenly saw who it was who'd been barking back at me!

Tyler meets Tyson

Sarah had another little dog with her – but guess what? The dog looked like me! I sort of said, "Hello," with an uncertain little wag of my tail, and Sarah then introduced us, saying, "Tyler this is Tyson."

"Hmm, Tyson," I thought to myself, "not only does this new dog look like me, but his name sounds just like mine too!"

Tyson and I slowly walked towards each other and met nose to nose, followed by some suitable doggy-sniffing as we checked one another out. We looked so alike it was as if I was looking in a mirror! We each gave approving little wags of our tails, which Dad and Sarah thought meant we were pleased to meet one another, but really we were just wagging our tails because we were nervous and excited! Anyway, we both decided pretty quickly that the best thing to do was run off and chase one another around the garden and get to know each other.

Later on when we were eating our dinner, I overheard Sarah and Dad chatting in the kitchen. Sarah told Dad how she met Tyson, and that there was a pet rescue centre near to where she now lived, which was just like ours. They needed lots of volunteers to help walk the dogs each day, so whenever Sarah had some free time from the Army she had offered to be Tyson's 'walker'.

It wasn't long before she discovered how much she liked Tyson, and eventually she asked the rescue centre if she could be his new owner and take him home.

A New Friend for Sarah and Tyler

I didn't ask Tyson how old he was, but I don't think he was a brand new puppy dog. But just like poor old Tweedy, nobody had wanted him when he was born and he'd been stuck in the pet rescue centre for a very long time. I don't think he knew just how lucky he was that Sarah had chosen him too, but I told him that it wouldn't be long before he found out. Now there were three of us who'd been chosen by Sarah, and if you count Monty – that makes four! Talk about getting lucky!

Later that evening Tyson and I were having a little snooze by the fire while Dad cooked Sarah's favourite dinner. I heard her telling Dad that she could only stay for a few days but that she'd made plans for Dad's birthday by organising a party the following weekend. I'd never been to a birthday party before so I was quite excited about this, but then Sarah got a little sad as she explained that she'd have to leave again the day after Dad's party.

Sarah often went away with the Army now, but this time she had to go away for a very long time on what is called a 'tour of duty'. Sarah was worried about Tyson and said that she didn't want to put him back in the rescue shelter while she was away, which would break his little heart, so she asked Dad if Tyson could stay with us. Well, both of our ears stood up on end twitching away as we waited anxiously to hear Dad's response, and, to our delight, he agreed, saying, "That's no problem, Sarah, I'd love to have Tyson stay for a while; he and Tyler have almost got the same name and they look like brothers too - they'd be great company for each other."

With another great big hug Sarah said "Thanks Dad, I knew you would"

Learning to Swim

Over the next few days we had a great time with Sarah, and almost every day she took us out somewhere different for long walks. When Dad told her about the time I'd fallen into that horrible ditch, she decided to take us both to the river and taught us how to swim. Sarah didn't want either of us to get into that kind of trouble again, but what messy pups we were when we got home! Every day we were either soaking wet from the river or covered in mud from the fields. Dad seemed to spend more time bathing us than he did doing anything else!

Sarah's few days at home went very quickly, and the day she had to leave wasn't far away. But for now, no one was thinking about that – we were all really looking forward to Dad's birthday party!

Before she'd arrived home Sarah had already started organising everything by phoning family, friends, and neighbours; telling them we were going to have a great big party because this was a special birthday for Dad. I asked Tweedy if she knew how old Dad was, but she said she couldn't count that high, but she did think it was a very big number!

That night, as Tyson and I sat cuddled up either side of Sarah, she told Dad about all the exciting things she was doing in her new job with the Army, as well as all the plans she had for his birthday. But eventually Sarah said she was tired and used that as an excuse to go to bed early, but we both knew why she really wanted to go upstairs. It was time to wrap Dad's present!

Let's get this Party Started

The following day some of Dad's neighbours brought over lots of party food and others came to help set everything up. Because it was such a lovely, hot day Sarah decided we should have the party in the garden, but we didn't have enough chairs for everyone to sit on, so Sarah took some bales of hay from Monty's stable and laid them in a big circle in the corner of the garden! Monty didn't seem to mind, and we all thought it was a great idea!

Finally, everything was ready, so Sarah and our neighbours went inside to get themselves all dressed up for the party. Dad needed to go into town that morning and only just made it home when his friends and relatives started arriving for the party. He looked really happy that Sarah had done all of this for him, and was so pleased to see lots of people waiting for him in the garden. As the party began, everyone gave him cards and presents and then tucked into the lovely food that Sarah and our neighbours had prepared.

Tyson and I were having lots of fun rushing around and playing, but it was too much for Tweedy and she escaped by running up a tree! Monty was smiling away and really seemed to be enjoying all the party fun too, but Dad thought he might be feeling just a little bit left out of things because his tail was swishing away and he was kicking his stable door to get our attention. Then Dad had a good idea – because Monty was such a friendly horse he opened the stable door and let him out to wander amongst the party guests! Everyone made such a fuss of him and Monty thoroughly enjoyed being the centre of attention!

Monty gives Pony Rides!

There were quite a few children at the party too, so Sarah put Monty's saddle on so he could give them a little ride down the lane. Even some of the grown-up's tried to ride Monty, but apart from Dad and Sarah no one could ride him as well as me!

The party was so much fun and it really was a perfect day, but now it was time for Sarah to bring out Dad's birthday cake!

Everyone gathered around – including Monty – and as Sarah lit the candles we all began to sing "Happy Birthday to you - Happy Birthday to you", as loud as we could.

Just as Dad was taking in a deep breath so he could blow out his candles, Sarah shouted out, "Make a wish Dad!" I could see that Dad's eyes seemed to have little tears in them even though it was his party and he should be having lots of fun, so I ran over and wagged my tail and held up both of my paws to make him feel better. But I didn't know that people can sometimes have a little cry even when they're happy! Dad laughed at me and said, "I'm okay Tyler," and patted me on my head. After he'd made his secret wish to himself, Dad took in another really big, deep breath, and while everyone started to cheer he blew and blew as hard as he could until all of the candles were out!

Sarah gave Dad a special cake knife, and as he was about to cut a slice for everyone, they all burst out singing again! "Happy Birthday to you, Happy Birthday to you, Happy Birthday dear 'Dad', Happy Birthday to you"!

We were hoping we'd get some of that delicious-looking cake too, so we sat side by side wagging our tails like mad and making some really strange noises, which was as close to the singing as we could get! Tweedy was still up in the tree, but as she could see we'd finally stopped fooling around, she decided it was safe to come down to see if there was any party food she might like to eat! As she slowly walked closer and closer towards us, I could see that Tyson had his eye on her – he hadn't got to know her well enough yet, so he wanted to chase her right back up the tree! But just as he was thinking of putting his little plan into action, Tyson nudged me and whispered, "Oh-oh." He'd been spotted – Sarah was looking straight at us both with that, 'now, you two behave' stare in her eyes! We both felt a little guilty because Dad was just about to cut his cake, so we thought we'd fall in line for just a few more minutes!

As Dad looked around at the people in the garden he said a big 'thank you' to everyone for their cards and presents, and then with a big smile on his face he gazed down at his birthday cake. I could see another little 'happy' tear in his eyes as he stopped for a moment before slicing into the cake to read once more the special words Sarah had written on it.

Happy Birthday
To the Best Dad in the World

XXXOOOXXX

Written in loving memory of

Corporal Sarah Louise Bryant (Née Feely)

British Army Intelligence Corps

Born 17/12/1981

KIA Afghanistan 17/06/2008

R.I.P.

LV123499
29 October 2009
LaVergne, TN USA